GALE

CENGAGE Learning

Novels for Students, Volume 37

Project Editor: Sara Constantakis Rights Acquisition and Management: Margaret Chamberlain-Gaston, Jackie Jones Composition: Evi Abou-El-Seoud Manufacturing: Rhonda Dover

Imaging: John Watkins

Product Design: Pamela A. E. Galbreath, Jennifer Wahi Content Conversion: Katrina Coach Product Manager: Meggin Condino © 2011 Gale, Cengage Learning

For product information and technology assistance, contact us at **Gale Customer Support, 1-800-877-4253.**

For permission to use material from this text or product, submit all requests online at <u>www.cengage.com/permissions</u>.

Further permissions questions can be emailed to **permissionrequest@cengage.com** While every effort has been made to ensure the reliability of the information presented in this publication, Gale, a part of Cengage Learning, does not guarantee the accuracy of the data contained herein. Gale accepts no payment for listing; and inclusion in the publication of any organization, agency, institution, publication, service, or individual does not imply endorsement of the editors or publisher. Errors brought to the attention of the publisher and verified to the satisfaction of the publisher will be corrected in future editions.

Gale
27500 Drake Rd.
Farmington Hills, MI, 48331-3535

ISBN-13: 978-1-4144-6700-9
ISBN-10: 1-4144-6700-1
ISSN 1094-3552

This title is also available as an e-book.

ISBN-13: 978-1-4144-7366-6
ISBN-10: 1-4144-7366-4
Contact your Gale, a part of Cengage Learning sales
representative for ordering information.

Printed in Mexico
1 2 3 4 5 6 7 15 14 13 12 11

Holes

Louis Sachar 1998

Introduction

Holes, published in 1998, has become one of the most frequently taught young-adult novels in American middle and high schools. It was the first book to win both the National Book Award for Young People's Literature (1998) and the Newbery Medal (1999), which recognizes the most distinguished contribution to American children's literature; as of 2010, no other book had captured both awards. *Holes* has been adapted as both a film and a stage play, and has sold more than five million copies in at least fifteen languages, including English, Spanish, Japanese, and Chinese.

The story deals with Stanley Yelnats, a fifteen-year-old boy who is sent to Camp Green Lake, a boot camp for wayward boys, for a crime he did not commit. At the camp, boys spend hours each day in the hot Texas sun, digging large holes in the desert in a program that is supposed to build character. As the novel tells what happens to Stanley there, it weaves in tall tales featuring the ancestors of several of the present-day characters. *Holes* is striking for its humor, and also for its insightful portrayal of young men who need a second chance, of the power of friendship, and of the importance of family.

Author Biography

Sachar was born in East Meadow, New York, on March 20, 1954. An only child, he moved with his parents to Orange County, California, when he was nine years old, and graduated from high school there. He was a strong student, good at math and excited about reading and writing. He spent one year at Antioch College in Yellow Springs, Ohio, but when his father died, he transferred to the University of California at Berkeley to be nearer to his mother. At one point in his college career, Sachar needed three credits to satisfy a requirement, and he signed up to be a teacher's aide because it looked like an easy way to complete the credits. He had no particular interest in teaching or in young people when he began, but he took to the children quickly, and they liked him. Sachar began writing a series of humorous stories about schoolchildren, naming the characters after kids at the school where he worked. Shortly after graduating from college, he learned that his first book, *Sideways Stories from Wayside School* (1978), had been accepted for publication.

By this time, Sachar was enrolled in law school at the University of California at San Francisco. He completed his law degree in 1980 and began practicing law part-time in 1981, but he continued writing, and tried to decide which way his career path would take him. In 1983, he visited Texas as part of a promotional tour for his second book, and met Clara Askew, a school counselor, whom he married in 1985. The couple have one child, a daughter named Sherre, born in 1987. They spent their early years as a couple in San Francisco; Carla continued to work in education, and her husband quit his law practice to write full-time. His fourth novel, *There's a Boy in the Girls' Bathroom* (1987), won several awards, and established Sachar as an important writer of humorous and insightful books about middle-school-aged misfits. He has written several books for children, including five books in the Wayside School series and eight novels about a third-grade boy named Marvin Redpost.

In 1990, the Sachar family moved to Austin, Texas, where they lived as of 2010. It was there, faced with the relentless Texas heat, that Sachar wrote his most important novel, and his first one for young adults, *Holes*, in 1998. The book enjoyed great critical and popular success, winning both the National Book Award and the Newbery Medal. Sachar followed the novel with two sequels and a film version, for which he wrote the screenplay. Between 2000 and 2009, much of Sachar's time was consumed with projects related to *Holes*, but 2010 saw the publication of *The Cardturner*, a young-adult novel about a teen who gets involved in one of Sachar's favorite hobbies: playing bridge.

Chapters 1–6

Holes opens with a description of Camp Green Lake, a dried-up lake bed in Texas with little shade. The narrator addresses the reader directly, explaining that the one shady spot—a hammock between two trees—belongs to the Warden, and warning readers to beware of rattlesnakes, scorpions and, especially, the dreaded yellow-spotted lizards, whose bite is always fatal. It is not until the second chapter that the protagonist, Stanley Yelnats V, is introduced. Stanley, the narrator explains, was given a choice by a judge: go to jail or go to Camp Green Lake. Stanley is an unpopular, overweight middle-school kid who comes from an unlucky but optimistic family. They trace their bad luck to Stanley's "no-good-dirty-rotten-pig-stealing-great-great-grandfather," who brought a curse down on the family generations ago. Now, Stanley's inventor father is unable to find any success, and Stanley has been sent to Camp Green Lake for eighteen months for a crime he did not commit.

The story moves back and forth between the past and the present, introducing Stanley's ancestors and their fates. But the focus in these chapters is on Stanley's arrival at Camp Green Lake after a long bus ride across a barren landscape. The first person he meets there is Mr. Sir, who issues him two sets of orange clothing, a towel, and a canteen, and tells him how he will spend his time at the camp: every day he must dig a hole five feet deep and five feet across. When his hole is completed each day, his work is done and he may relax any way he chooses. Stanley is assigned to D tent, and introduced to his counselor, Mr. Pendanski. He also meets the six other boys who live in D tent, including Armpit, X-Ray, and Zero, as they return from digging. After a shower and dinner, Stanley lies down on his cot, thinking of the day not long before when, as he was walking home from school, a pair of sneakers fell out of the sky and hit him on the head. The sneakers turned out to be a pair donated for a homeless shelter fund raiser, and Stanley was sent to Camp Green Lake as punishment for stealing them.

Media Adaptations

- *Holes* was adapted as a film starring Shia LaBeouf and Sigourney

Weaver, with the screenplay by Sachar. It was released by Walt Disney Pictures in 2003 and is distributed on DVD.

- Listening Library produced an unabridged audio edition of *Holes* in 2006. Read by Kerry Bever, it is available on CD or as an MP3 download.

Chapters 7–9

On Stanley's first day at Camp Green Lake, he rises at 4:30, has breakfast, and heads out with the others to dig his first hole. He sees that the area around the camp is covered with holes and with mounds of the dirt that came out of the holes. Each camper is shown where to dig each day, with the added warning that "anything interesting or unusual" must be given to the authorities. However, the boys are made to understand that they are not looking for anything in particular; they dig holes simply to build character. Stanley begins to dig in the hard earth, and blisters form on his hands almost immediately. Mr. Sir brings the boys water partway through the day, and when he takes a break, Stanley can see that he is digging much more slowly than the others. As the day goes on, the sun becomes hotter, and Stanley's blisters burst and re-form. Zero, a skinny quiet boy, is the first to finish, and all the rest of the boys finish well before Stanley does.

With his last bit of strength, Stanley climbs out of the hole, spits into it, and walks back to camp.

He takes a shower, using his allotted four minutes of water, and heads to the recreation room, where the boys can watch a broken TV, play with broken games, or just hang out. Stanley writes a letter to his mother, lying about the fun he is having at camp. Zero, who rarely speaks and whom everyone else ignores because he is quiet and strange, asks Stanley if the shoes he found had red *X*'s on the back, but only stares when Stanley tells him that they did. The boys head off to dinner.

Interwoven with Stanley's first day is the story of his great-great-grandfather Elya Yelnats, who lived in Latvia. As a teenager, he fell in love with Myra Menke. To win her, he needed to beat out a pig farmer who also wanted to marry her, and who could offer Myra's family a fat pig in exchange for her hand. Elya turned to Madame Zeroni, an Egyptian, for advice. She gave him a baby pig and instructed him to carry it to the top of a mountain every day and let it drink from a stream there. By Myra's fifteenth birthday, the pig would be the fattest pig around, and he could win Myra's hand. Then, he was to carry Madame Zeroni to the top of the mountain and let her drink from the stream. If he failed to do this, he and his descendants would be cursed. On Myra's birthday, each man brought a pig, and the two pigs were found to weigh exactly the same amount. Myra, who was rather stupid and unable to decide which man to marry, asked them to pick a number between one and ten. Disgusted, Elya walked away.

He signed on as a deck hand, and came to America to start over, forgetting that he had promised to carry Madame Zeroni up the mountain. He settled in America, learned English, got married and tried to be a farmer, but lightning kept striking his barn and wiping out his crops. He searched for Madame Zeroni's son, supposedly settled in America, so that he could somehow settle his debt to the family, but never found him. In a few years his son, the first Stanley Yelnats, was born.

Chapters 10–15

Stanley digs his second hole, which proves to be much harder than the first because of his sore muscles and torn-up hands. X-Ray urges Stanley to give him anything "interesting" he might find, so X-Ray can turn it in and get a day off as a reward; Stanley agrees, wanting to fit in with the more experienced boys. That night, Mr. Pendanski, whom the boys call "Mom," leads the boys in a discussion about their future when they leave Camp Green Lake. He tries to make the boys accept responsibility for the misdeeds that got them sent to the camp, and to think about what they like to do. He belittles Zero, calling him "not completely worthless," earning Zero's angry stare.

As the days pass, the digging gets easier. One day, Stanley does find something interesting in his hole, a gold tube with a heart and the letters *K* and *B* engraved on it. He gives it to X-Ray, and encourages him to wait until the following morning to turn it in, so he will get more of the day off as a reward. X-Ray rewards Stanley with a more favored place in the line for water, and Stanley, who never had friends at school, begins to feel more accepted by the others. The next morning, X-Ray shows the tube to Mr. Pendanski, who summons the Warden to see it. The Warden turns out to be Mrs. Walker, a tall red-haired woman, who is excited by the find and sets all the boys to digging near X-Ray's hole. Only Stanley knows exactly where he was digging the day before, when the tube was actually found, and knows that today's dig is far away.

Chapters 16–22

After a few more days, the Warden becomes discouraged because the boys do not find anything else of interest. Stanley gets a letter from his mother, which tells him that his father's experiments with ways to recycle old sneakers are creating an awful stink. As Stanley is writing back to her, Zero confesses that he does not know how to read and asks Stanley to teach him. But Stanley does not have the energy, and refuses.

One day, one of the boys steals Mr. Sir's bag of sunflower seeds from the water truck, and as they are passing it around Stanley drops it. He accepts the blame for stealing the bag, and is taken to see the Warden for his punishment. The Warden is not interested in Mr. Sir's sunflower seeds, and takes from her makeup bag a special nail polish made with rattlesnake venom; she scratches Mr. Sir's face with it, raising horrible welts. When Stanley is taken back to his hole by the furious Mr. Sir, he finds that Zero, the fastest digger of the group, has almost finished it for him. The two boys agree that Stanley will teach Zero to read in exchange for help with digging his holes. That night, thinking about the Warden and her makeup bag, Stanley realizes that the gold tube he found was part of a lipstick case. Remembering that his great-grandfather Stanley Yelnats, who had made a fortune in the stock market, had once been robbed in the desert by the outlaw Kissin' Kate Barlow, he wonders if the lipstick case could have been hers.

Chapters 23–28

Now the narrator flashes back one hundred and ten years, to a time when Green Lake was actually a lake. Miss Katherine Barlow was a schoolteacher, famous for her beauty and her spiced peaches. The richest man in town was stupid and arrogant Trout Walker. Walker expected to marry Miss Katherine, but she had no interest in him. Instead, she favored Sam, an African American man who sold sweet onions that had the power to cure illness. Sam had a little rowboat and an old donkey, Mary Lou. He was strong and smart, and he helped Miss Katherine make repairs on her schoolhouse in exchange for jars of spiced peaches. One day, the two were seen kissing. Drunk and angry, Trout Walker led an angry mob who burned down the school and killed Sam and Mary Lou. Miss Katherine became the outlaw Kissin' Kate Barlow, who left a lipstick imprint of a kiss on the foreheads of all the men she killed. And no rain fell on Green Lake for the next one hundred ten years. Twenty years after Sam's death, Kate returned to Green Lake, now a ghost town. Trout Walker and his wife found her, and demanded at gunpoint that she tell them where she had buried her loot. She walked them out to the center of the dried-up lake bed, but before she could tell them anything, she was bitten by a yellow-spotted lizard and died, laughing.

Back at Camp Green Lake, Mr. Sir's face swells horribly, and he takes out his pain and anger on Stanley, pouring his share of water on the ground instead of into his canteen. Stanley begins teaching Zero to read, beginning with the alphabet and then teaching him to write his name. Zero tells Stanley that his real name is not Zero, but Hector Zeroni.

Chapters 29–36

The weather gets hotter and more humid at Camp Green Lake, making the digging even harder. One day, a flash of lightning in the distance makes a rock formation look like a giant thumb, and Stanley remembers the family legend that his great-grandfather, after being robbed but not killed by Kissin' Kate Barlow, "found refuge on God's thumb." After forty-five days of digging, Stanley is leaner and stronger than he has ever been, but the other boys begin to resent the help he is getting from Zero, and the harmony among the white, black, and Hispanic boys begins to dissolve. During a fistfight, Zero comes to Stanley's aid, and nearly strangles another boy. Mr. Pendanski hears about the reading lessons and mocks Zero for being too stupid to learn anything. At the end of his rope, Zero hits Mr. Pendanski in the face with his shovel, and runs away across the lake. No one chases him; they know he will have to come back soon for water. But he does not come back. After a few days, the Warden has all of Zero's files destroyed so there will be no record of him, and another boy is brought in to fill his place.

Stanley cannot forget Zero, and feels guilty that he did not try to help him. A few days later, on impulse, he steals Mr. Sir's truck, but not knowing how to drive, he promptly drives the truck into one of the holes. Like Zero, he takes off. After hours of walking, he comes across an upside-down boat, the *Mary Lou*, and finds Zero hiding beneath it. Zero has stayed alive by eating from a cache of canning jars filled with what he calls "Sploosh," a sweet mush that tastes faintly of peaches. Zero refuses to go back to camp, so the two boys head toward the rock formation that resembles a thumb, taking the last four jars of Sploosh with them. Zero has been eating the Sploosh for days, and his stomach begins to cramp painfully, but he and Stanley manage to reach the steep mountains.

Chapters 37–42

The boys move closer and closer to the Big

Thumb, climbing as they go. Finally they come to patches of weeds and swarms of bugs and realize they must be near water. But Zero's strength is gone; he can go no further. Stanley picks him up and carries him up the mountain until they reach a flat, muddy area. Digging for water, Stanley discovers that they are in a field of onions. The story flashes back to Sam and his donkey Mary Lou, and the first time Sam's onion tonic made a sick child well. Zero slowly regains his strength as he eats the onions, and he tells Stanley about his childhood.

Zero and his mother were homeless, and they often survived by stealing what they needed. In fact, it was Zero who stole the sneakers from the homeless shelter, not being able to read the sign that identified them as valuable shoes from a celebrity athlete. When the commotion started over the missing shoes, he went outside and set them on top of a parked car; he was arrested the next day when he stole another pair of shoes from a store. The shoes that Stanley was accused of stealing had, apparently, fallen off the car and onto Stanley's head when the car went over an overpass. Now the boys are alone on top of a mountain, with nothing to eat but onions, but Stanley feels glad for all he has been through and for the friend he has gained. And he develops a plan, asking Zero if he would like to "dig one more hole."

Chapters 43–50

The boys hike down the mountain, and Zero tells the rest of his story. He remembers standing in a crib in a yellow room before he and his mother became homeless, and he remembers that he used to wait for her in a playground structure during the day while she went off in search of food. One day, she did not come back, and he lived alone in the park for more than a month, sleeping in the playscape. The boys make their way back toward camp, and after the diggers leave for the day, the two go to the hole where Stanley found the lipstick tube. Digging through the night, they find a suitcase buried in the hole. They begin to climb out, but are surprised by the Warden shining a flashlight on them and thanking them for finding the suitcase. Mr. Sir and Mr. Pendanski arrive, but the adults are prevented from taking the case by the discovery that, along with the boys, there are several of the deadly yellow-spotted lizards. The Warden, who says she spent every weekend and holiday digging holes with her parents when she was a child, decides she can wait a little longer for the lizards to kill the boys, if it means she will finally have the suitcase. After the boys are dead, they can easily be buried in one of the holes.

As everyone waits to see what will happen next, the adults reveal that an attorney has come to the camp that day to get Stanley released; they know it will be difficult to make up a believable story about Stanley's running away and being bitten by the lizards. When the sun comes up, the attorney comes back and finds them all gathered around the hole. The Warden accuses the boys of sneaking into her cabin and stealing her suitcase, but Zero astonishes everyone when he shows that the suitcase has Stanley's name on it. The lizards move off, the boys crawl out of the hole, and Stanley and Zero are released into the attorney's custody, taking the suitcase with them.

Again, the novel flashes back to Sam the onion man. Two men from the town of Green Lake headed to the mountains to hunt rattlesnakes one day, and Sam gave them bottles of onion juice to drink before they went. The juice, he said, would protect them from yellow-spotted lizards, which "don't like onion blood."

Suddenly, things begin to look up. Stanley's father has successfully invented a product to eliminate stinky feet—a product that smells like spiced peaches. Rain falls on Green Lake. The suitcase, which was stolen from Stanley Yelnats by Kissin' Kate Barlow, is filled with jewelry and financial documents worth almost two million dollars. Zero is reunited with his mother. It may or may not all be due to Elya Yelnats's great-great-grandson Stanley having carried Madame Zeroni's great-great-great-grandson up a mountain.

Characters

Armpit

Armpit, whose given name is Theodore, is one of the campers in D tent. Armpit is tall, African American, and, after X-Ray, the second most senior boy in Group D. Armpit generally follows X-Ray's lead, befriending Stanley or turning on him when X-Ray does. He is tough, an unemotional survivor, but seems genuinely glad when Stanley and Zero turn up alive.

Katherine Barlow

Miss Katherine Barlow is a beautiful schoolteacher in the nineteenth-century town of Green Lake. She is good-hearted and generous, and famous for her canned spiced peaches. Every man in town, including the wealthy Trout Walker, wants to marry her, but she is in love with the African American onion peddler Sam. Flouting the law that prohibits romantic relationships across racial lines, Katherine and Sam kiss, and are seen by one of the townspeople. When a gang of angry white men kills Sam and burns down the schoolhouse, Katherine Barlow becomes the outlaw Kissin' Kate Barlow. Many people suspect that she has cursed the town of Green Lake because, after Samdies, rain stops falling in the area and the lake becomes a desert. For twenty years, she roams the West, robbing men and killing many of them. Those she kills she marks with the lipstick imprint of a kiss on their foreheads. Kissin' Kate is a successful robber, accumulating a great hoard of loot. She retires to a quiet cabin in Green Lake, by then a ghost town. But Trout Walker and his wife track her down, demanding the loot. Before she can tell them where she has buried it, she is bitten by a yellow-spotted lizard and dies, laughing. More than one hundred years later, Zero avoids death in the desert when he finds the last remaining jars of her spiced peaches, naming the substance "Sploosh."

Caveman

See Stanley Yelnats V

Derrick Dunne

Derrick Dunne is a bully who tormented Stanley every day at school. No one believed Stanley's accusations, because Derrick was much smaller than Stanley.

Kissin' Kate

See Katherine Barlow

Mary Lou

Mary Lou is the beloved donkey of Sam the onion peddler, and the namesake of his little boat.

Mom

See Mr. Pendanski

Myra Menke

Fourteen-year-old Myra Menke is the pretty but stupid Latvian girl who Stanley's great-great-grandfather Elya Yelnats falls in love with when he is fifteen. She is spoiled and delicate and useless, but Elya can see only her beauty, so he tries to win her hand in marriage. Myra's father agrees to give Myra to the man who offers the biggest pig, but on the appointed day, the pigs presented by Elya and his rival are equal in weight. Myra, not caring whom she marries, tells the men to each pick a number; Elya finally realizes she is stupid and indifferent, and walks away.

Mr. Pendanski

Mr. Pendanski is the counselor for Group D at Camp Lake Green. He sometimes acts kindly toward the boys, earning him the nickname "Mom," but he is also stern. He refuses to use the boys' nicknames because he wants to prepare them for how they will be received when they leave Camp Green Lake, and he leads a discussion to help them articulate their dreams for the future. But he is merciless to Zero, repeatedly calling him stupid and worthless. When he does this out where the boys are digging on a particularly hot day, Zero is finally pushed to hit Mr. Pendanski in the face with his shovel and run away. After Zero has been missing for a few days, Mr. Pendanski erases his file from Camp Green Lakes computers so there will be no record of his having ever been there.

Sam

Sam is an African American man who sells onions and an onion tonic in nineteenth-century Green Lake. With his donkey, Mary Lou, he delivers onions from a secret field across the lake, and his onions and tonic are said to cure diseases that medicine cannot touch. Sam is also handy with tools, and he fixes up the schoolhouse where Miss Katherine Barlow, the white schoolteacher, works. Sam is well liked by the people of Green Lake, but when he is seen kissing Miss Katherine, a line has been crossed. A gang of men come to lynch him, and Sam and Katherine try to escape across the lake in his boat, the *Mary Lou*. Sam is shot and killed out on the lake, and the boat sinks after Katherine is rescued from it.

Mr. Sir

Mr. Sir is the director of Camp Green Lake, second-in-command to the Warden. As the novel opens, he has recently given up smoking, and he chews on sunflower seeds to help him avoid cigarettes. He wears sunglasses and a cowboy hat and has a rattlesnake tattooed on his arm. He greets Stanley when he arrives at the camp, runs through the rules with him, and utters what will become a refrain for him: "This isn't a Girl Scout Camp." Mr. Sir is tough but fair, until the boys steal and spill his bag of sunflower seeds. Stanley takes the blame for the theft, and Mr. Sir delivers him to be punished by the Warden. But the Warden instead punishes Mr. Sir for wasting her time, scratching his face with her special nail polish made from rattlesnake venom. His face swells up painfully, and for the next several weeks he turns against Stanley, refusing to give him water when he brings it to the others. Mr. Sir is the one delivering water the day Stanley steals the truck and tries to get away, driving into a hole instead.

Squid

Squid is one of the boys in Group D at Camp Green Lake. Early in the book, he makes fun of Stanley for writing a letter to his mother. At the end, however, as Stanley is about to leave Camp Green Lake, Squid gives Stanley his mother's phone number and asks him to phone and tell her he is sorry for his past mistakes.

Stanley's mother

Stanley's mother is patient and kind, and continually optimistic. When Stanley or his father good-naturedly blame their bad luck on the curse brought down on their heads by the misdeeds of Stanley's "no-good-dirty-rotten-pig-stealing-great-great-grandfather," Stanley's mother, who does not believe in the curse, reminds them that Stanley

Yelnats once made a fortune investing in the stock market. Stanley's mother is a full-time homemaker, and puts up with her husband's smelly experiments and repeated failures. Stanley, her only child, lies to her about conditions at Green Lake Camp, pretending it is a fun recreation spot, so she will not worry about him there.

Charles "Trout" Walker

Charles Walker, nicknamed "Trout," is the son of the richest man in the county surrounding nineteenth-century Green Lake. He has earned the nickname "Trout" because his feet always smell like dead fish. Trout attends the evening adult classes taught by Miss Katherine Barlow, but he comes only to flirt with her or to make stupid jokes; he has no interest in learning. When Miss Katherine rejects Trout and chooses Sam instead, Trout leads the mob that burns the school and kills Sam. Twenty years later, he and his wife attempt to force Kissin' Kate to turn over her stolen loot, but all they learn is that it is buried somewhere in the desert. At the end of the book, it is made clear the Trout Walker is the grandfather or great-grandfather of the Warden, Ms. Walker, and that his descendants have spent their lives digging holes, looking for buried loot.

Ms. Walker

See The Warden

The Warden

The Warden is Ms. Walker, a tall red-haired woman who runs Camp Green Lake. She is strict and humorless, and neither the boys nor the staff members ever dare cross her. In fact, when Stanley first arrives at Camp Green Lake, Mr. Pendanski teaches him the camp's only rule: "Don't upset the Warden." She does not yell, but speaks her commands in a quiet, gentle voice, and even says, "Thank you"; still, when she tells Mr. Pendanski to refill the boys' canteens, he knows that she expects him to do it without questioning her authority. When Mr. Sir wastes her time with his complaint about his spilled sunflower seeds, she scratches his face with nail polish made with rattlesnake venom. She pokes Armpit with her pitchfork for taking a bathroom break, making three small puncture wounds in his chest. And when it appears that Zero has run away and probably died in the desert, she has no qualms about ordering his files destroyed so there will be no record of his having ever been at the camp. It is the Warden who has come up with the plan to have the boys dig holes to build character, with the warning that anything they dig up must be reported to her. After Stanley and Zero find the buried suitcase, the Warden reveals that she has been looking for it her entire life, that she grew up watching her parents "dig holes, every weekend and holiday." As she grew older, she dug, too, "even on Christmas." She is willing to watch the boys be killed by the yellow-spotted lizards if it means she will finally have the treasure. The thought that she could be so close to having the suitcase and still not get it—or even get to see inside it—is terrible for her.

X-Ray

X-Ray is the de facto leader of the boys in Group D. X-Ray's given name is Rex, but only Mr. Pendanski calls him that at Camp Green Lake. He has the nickname "X-Ray" because he wears thick glasses and still sees poorly. A large, tough African American boy, X-Ray determines how the boys line up when it is time for their water breaks, and he intimidates Stanley into letting him be the one who claims credit for finding the gold tube. Still, he looks after Stanley once Stanley has earned his trust, and the younger boy starts to feel for the first time that he has friends. But when X-Ray comes to see it as unfair that Zero helps Stanley dig his holes every day, he expresses his displeasure in racial terms, accusing the white Stanley of making the African American Zero his slave, and later mockingly insists Stanley stand at the front of the line for water since he feels he is better than the others. This taunting leads to a fight that ultimately leads to Zero striking Mr. Pendanski and running away.

Elya Yelnats

Elya Yelnats is Stanley's "dirty-rotten-pig-stealing-great-great-grandfather." As a fifteen-year-old boy in Latvia, he falls in love with Myra Menke, a beautiful but stupid girl. Myra's father has agreed that she will marry the man who brings him the fattest pig on Myra's fifteenth birthday. Elya consults his friend Madame Zeroni, who gives him a small pig and instructs him to carry it up the mountain each day to a special stream, until it grows fat and he grows strong. In exchange for the advice and the pig, he promises to carry Madame Zeroni up the mountain as well. He follows her advice and presents Myra Menke's father with a pig exactly as large as his rival's, and Myra decides to have the men pick a number to win her hand. Instead, Elya leaves for America to start over, forgetting his promise to Madame Zeroni. He marries, and fathers Stanley Yelnats, but he and his descendants are cursed to endure constant bad luck because of his forgotten promise.

Stanley Yelnats

The first Stanley Yelnats, Elya's son and the protagonist's great-grandfather, at first seemed to be proof that the family was not truly cursed. Stanley Yelnats made a fortune in the stock market. On his way west, however, he was robbed of his fortune by the outlaw Kissin' Kate Barlow. Kissin' Kate did not kill him, but left him stranded in the desert.

Stanley Yelnats II

Stanley Yelnats II is Stanley's father, an inventor who tries and tries but never succeeds, but who keeps his spirits high. He has recently been trying to invent something to make sneakers stop smelling, but all he has managed to do is stink up the family's apartment and get them threatened with eviction. On the day after Stanley carries Zero up the mountain, strengthened by Katherine Barlow's spiced peaches, Stanley's father invents a peach-scented product that stops foot odor. It is his first successful product. With the money Stanley V ultimately gets from the contents of the buried suitcase, he buys his family a new house with a laboratory for his father.

Stanley Yelnats V

Stanley Yelnats V is a white, overweight, unpopular middle-school boy, and the main character of the novel. Although he is well loved at home, he is bullied at school, and he seems to be followed by bad luck that makes his inability to stand up for himself even worse. Walking home from school one day, he is suddenly hit on the head by a pair of sneakers that seem to have fallen from the sky. No one believes this version of the events, and he is sentenced to Camp Green Lake for the theft. At the camp he is assigned to Group D with other boys who have committed crimes. From the beginning, Stanley struggles to fit in with this new group of tough, cynical young men, but when he accidentally bumps into a boy from another tent, he earns the nickname "Caveman" and some grudging respect as a good fighter. At first, Stanley's low expectations for his own life serve him well; the digging, the blisters, the four-minute showers, and the bad food are no more than he expects, so although he suffers, he does not rebel. As the days go by, Stanley becomes physically and mentally stronger. He does what he can to get along: he lets X-Ray take the credit for digging up a gold tube, he takes the blame for spilling Mr. Sir's sunflower seeds, and he learns to keep his mouth shut and do what the adults tell him. He keeps his promise to his mother and writes her a letter every week, but he lies to make the camp seem like fun. And he tells no one when he figures out what the gold tube is, and when he remembers where it was actually found.

It takes Stanley a while to realize that although Zero cannot read, he is actually quite smart. When Stanley begins to think for himself where Zero is concerned, and goes out of his way to teach Zero to read, he makes his first real friend. Later, when Zero runs away and seems to be in danger, Stanley is the only one to take action to save him: he tries to steal a truck, but ends up following Zero across the desert on foot. He finds Zero, and the two boys make their way to a rock formation that Stanley calls God's Thumb, where his great-grandfather may have taken refuge decades before. Zero becomes ill, and Stanley uses his muscles and his brain to get them both to safety. He carries Zero up the mountain, finds water and digs for it, uncovers the onions, and makes a plan for finding Kissin' Kate Barlow's hidden loot. The boys find the buried suitcase—and a nest full of poisonous lizards. When it appears that Stanley has a chance to be rescued and taken away from Green Lake Camp by the attorney who appears suddenly, he will not leave

Zero behind, so the attorney is forced to look into Zero's case as well. Stanley is rewarded for his loyalty and intelligence with a suitcase full of treasure, a new home for his family, the restoration of his honor, and a new best friend.

Zero

Zero is a small, quiet African American boy at Camp Green Lake, one of the boys in Group D. He has a long skinny neck and wild blond hair, and he almost never speaks. The other boys pay him little attention, thinking that he is "one weird dude," but Mr. Pendanski taunts Zero mercilessly, making fun of him for being stupid and worthless. In fact, Zero is naturally intelligent and quite good at math, but as the reader learns later, he has had little formal education because he and his mother were homeless for many years. He has never heard of *Sesame Street* or common nursery rhymes, and he cannot read or write. He does have one useful skill, however: he loves to dig, and is by far the fastest holedigger at Camp Green Lake.

Slowly, Zero and Stanley become friends. The first time Zero asks Stanley to teach him to read, Stanley rejects him, and goes over to join the more popular boys. But he does begin to give Zero reading lessons in exchange for help digging holes, and Zero learns quickly. When Stanley gets into a fistfight one day, Zero jumps in to defend his friend, although he is much smaller than the other boys. Stanley repays this loyalty when he runs off to find

Zero in the desert. Together, the boys learn to work together, and so save their lives. It is Zero who finds the upturned boat and the Sploosh, and who reads the name "Stanley Yelnats" on the once-buried suitcase, and it is Stanley who finds the water and the onions, and who carries Zero to the top of the mountain. As they hike, Zero tells Stanley about his past: his dim memory of a yellow bedroom, his years of homelessness, how he and his mother used to steal to survive, how he was arrested for stealing a pair of shoes. He confesses that he was the one who stole the shoes the Stanley was convicted of stealing, and reveals that his real name is Hector Zeroni. (Neither he nor Stanley realizes that he is the direct descendant of Madame Zeroni, or that the two friends have fulfilled Stanley's ancestor's promise and ended the curse.) In the end, Zero is rewarded for his perseverance, his loyalty and his courage in the way fairy-tale heroes are rewarded: he becomes rich and is reunited with his mother.

Hector Zeroni

See Zero

Madame Zeroni

Madame Zeroni is an old Egyptian woman who lives at the edge of the Latvian town where Elya Yelnats lives. She has dark, exotic looks and only one foot, and she has a store of old stories that Elya loves to listen to. She tries to help Elya win Myra's hand, advising him to carry a pig up the mountain each day and then present the pig to Myra's father. In exchange, she makes Elya promise to carry her up the mountain as well and let her drink from a stream there and sing to him. When Elya forgets to do this part of his task, she curses him and his descendants for all eternity.

Friendship

The most important lesson Stanley Yelnats learns in *Holes* is the power of friendship. It is not a lesson he learns grudgingly; he yearns for friendship, although he may not be able to articulate that feeling. Before he came to Camp Green Lake, he was continually bullied at school. Although his parents were loving and attentive, "He didn't have any friends at home," and as he rides the bus to Camp Green Lake he thinks, "Maybe he'd make some friends." Of course, to have a friend one must be a friend, and Stanley has had little or no practice at this. When Zero first asks Stanley to teach him to read, he refuses. Zero is generally thought of as worthless and weird, and Stanley desperately wants to fit in with the boys in Group D. He decides that, after a long day of digging, he had better "save his energy for the people who counted" instead of wasting it on Zero. The narrator comments that it is not only Stanley's muscles that have gotten tougher through all the digging—"His heart had hardened as well."

Over time, though, Stanley learns how to be a friend. At first, when he does seemingly selfless things like turning over the gold tube to X-Ray or taking the blame for stealing the sunflower seeds, he is only doing them to gain acceptance; he expects to gain more than he gives up in these transactions. But when he begins to teach Zero to read, he is taking his first steps toward kindness, and that kindness is quickly repaid when Zero jumps in to defend Stanley during a fistfight. After Zero runs away, Stanley realizes that he should have coached Zero without asking for anything in return. When he sets out to save Zero, risking his own safety, it is out of friendship only, not for any gain. The two boys survive physical hardship in the desert and in the mountains through trust and cooperation— through friendship. If Zero did not share the Sploosh, if Stanley did not share the water and onions, they would starve. If Stanley had not taught Zero to read, Zero would not be able to identify the suitcase's owner. And if Stanley did not insist that he would not leave Camp Green Lake without Zero, Zero would surely be harmed. Both boys, who through no fault of their own, have spent their lives depending only on themselves, learn about friendship, and they are rewarded with money, security, and love.

Ancestry

A common theme in literature is the idea that future generations continue to pay for the mistakes that people make. This idea, that children continue to pay for the mistakes of their ancestors, runs throughout *Holes*. In Stanley's family, there is the curse laid upon Stanley's "no-good-dirty-rotten-pig-stealing-great-great-grandfather," Elya Yelnats, who failed to fulfill his promise to Madame Zeroni. Ever since Elya sailed to America, bad luck has followed the family. Elya was a hard-working farmer, but lightning kept striking his crops before he could harvest them; Stanley Yelnats made a fortune in the stock market, but had it all stolen by Kissin' Kate Barlow; Stanley's father fails repeatedly to invent something useful and profitable; Stanley is bullied at school and has the bad luck to be caught with a valuable pair of sneakers that fall out of the sky and hit himon the head. Although the Yelnats clan works hard and remains cheerfully optimistic, they seem to have been "doomed for all of eternity" by the curse. When Stanley fulfills Elya's promise by carrying Zero up a mountain, the curse is broken, and the new line of good luck extends backwards through the generations. Stanley finds the buried treasure, his father has his first success as an inventor, and Stanley the First's wealth is recovered.

Topics for Further Study

- After watching the film version of *Holes*, write an essay in which you compare how Stanley is portrayed in the book and in the film. Do the differences change how you perceive Stanley and what he goes through? You may wish to examine another character instead, for example, Sam the onion man or Mr. Pendanski.

- Using characters from the history of your school or your town, write a folk tale or a tall tale. If the resources are available, adapt the tale into a short video, and post it on You Tube or on your school's Web site.

- The novel *Holes* reveals some of the background of what Stanley, Zero, and the Warden were doing before they all met at Camp Green Lake. Choose another character—perhaps one of the other boys in Group D, or Zero's mother, or Mr. Sir or Mr. Pendanski—and write a five-minute monologue in that character's own voice, explaining what she or he was doing before appearing "on stage" in this novel. Read or recite your speech to your class.

- Read the young-adult novel, *Hoppergrass*, by Chris Carlton

Brown. Fifteen-year-old Browser gets sent to the Hill, an institution for troubled teens. Create a chart that compares the characters in *Holes* with the characters in *Hoppergrass*. Provide an explanation of why you think each set of characters is a match.

- Using Gliffy.com or another diagramming program, create a map of Camp Green Lake and the surrounding area. In another color or another layer, make a map of the same area as it appeared before the rains stopped.

- Visit the online bulletin board that Scholastic, the publisher of *Holes*, has created for kids to discuss the novel, and read several of the discussion threads. Post a comment on one interesting thread. With a group, come up with a new question that you believe will generate a lot of responses. Write a report in which you describe your process for brainstorming and choosing a question, and summarize the online responses.

The curse can be broken because Zero is also part of a long line. He is a direct descendant of

Madame Zeroni, the dark-skinned Egyptian woman who somehow made her way to Latvia. They share the same wide mouth (as does Zero's mother), and Madame Zeroni's eyes "seemed to expand" when she looked intensely at someone, just as Zero's do when Mr. Pendanski taunts him. Across the generations, Zero's family and Stanley's are connected by the song that Stanley learned from his father and Zero's mother learned from her grandmother: "*If only, if only.*"

Even the Warden is bound to her fate through her family tree. She is descended from Charles "Trout" Walker, the man who led the mob attack on Sam and the school, and the man who watched Kissin' Kate die before she could reveal where she had buried her loot. Apparently, his descendants have been digging holes ever since. The Warden remembers that her parents dug every weekend and holiday when she was a child, and that she joined them when she was old enough. This knowledge makes the Warden seem a bit more sympathetic; after all, the forces of family and destiny are powerful in this novel.

Race Relations

Race is an important element in the story, always underlying the action although it is seldom discussed directly. Stanley, like many people his age, is less conscious of race than his elders might be. When he meets Squid and X-Ray for the first time, for example, "their faces were so dirty that it took Stanley a moment to notice that one kid was white and the other black." After that comment, Stanley does not take much notice of their color. When he meets the other boys in tent D, their race and color are not identified by the narrator, and it may take readers several chapters to realize that Zero, with his "wild frizzy blond hair that stuck out in all directions," is black. In fact, although the boys of Group D are unusually diverse—three of them are African American, three are white, and one is Hispanic—they almost never discuss race. As Stanley observes, "On the lake they were all the same reddish brown color—the color of dirt." There is the possibility of racial tension when X-Ray and the others complain about Zero's helping Stanley dig his holes, and one of the boys taunts Stanley by calling Zero his "slave," but it is just part of the normal bad-mouthing that goes on among them, and within seconds they have moved on from calling Stanley a slave-master to saying that he thinks he is better than all of them. For the boys, race is not a divisive factor. And the only way Stanley and Zero survive in the desert is by working together, sharing everything equally.

But in the town of Green Lake a century before, race was much more prominent. Sam the onion man was respected because of his ability to cure illnesses, and generally liked because of his charm, but he was not allowed to attend the school because he was not an equal member of the society. Sam, an African American, is killed because he and Miss Katherine, a white woman, fall in love. As the sheriff explains, "It's against the law for a Negro to kiss a white woman." Katherine declares, "We're all equal under the eyes of God," and while the readers are meant to agree with her, the townspeople do not. Twice, people of Green Lake tell Miss Katherine, "God will punish you," and she does suffer the pain of losing Sam. But the town is also punished for its intolerance when the rains stop falling, the lake dries up, and the entire town disappears.

Style

Flashback

Holes relies heavily on flashbacks, or scenes depicting events that happened before the beginning of the main story. How Stanley Yelnats V is sent to and emerges triumphant from Camp Green Lake is the main narrative in the novel, occupying the story's "present." But in order for readers to understand the implications and the causes of Stanley's story, Sachar also tells several stories from the past: Elya Yelnats's quest to marry Myra Menke and his unfulfilled promise to Madame Zeroni in Latvia; Stanley Yelnats the First's success in the stock market and his subsequent robbery and stranding in the desert; Katherine Barlow's story of love, loss, and revenge; and Hector Zeroni's story of his life as a homeless petty thief. Sachar tells Stanley's story in roughly chronological order, from the time he arrives in Camp Green Lake to the end, with a small flashback to explain how he found the valuable sneakers falling from the sky. But the other flashbacks come in as the narrator feels compelled to give background information, often called exposition, without regard for chronology. Thus, readers do not learn until Chapter 49, after Stanley and Zero have left Camp Green Lake, that the secret to keeping yellow-spotted lizards from biting is to consume a lot of onions—something Sam the onion seller knew all along.

If Sachar or his narrator had told all of the pieces of the various narratives in chronological order, from the early days in Latvia to the day a year and a half after Stanley and Zero uncovered the buried suitcase, readers would have been denied delightful surprises. They would know as soon as the boys find the field of onions that eating them will be protection from the lizards. They would know before Stanley finds the shoes that Zero is the one who stole them. And they would know right away when Stanley's father invents his successful peach-scented odor remover, instead of learning about it when Stanley does. By using flashbacks, the novelist is able to parcel out information as he pleases, juxtaposing elements to highlight—or conceal—connections.

Tall Tale

While much of the material in *Holes* is realistic —sometimes grimly so—there are also elements of magic or fantasy. The story of Elya Yelnats in Latvia sounds very much like a typical fairy-tale or folk tale, with a suitor given a challenge by the father of his intended bride, a special stream on top of a mountain, and a curse laid on Elya and all his descendants by a one-legged Gypsy woman. Generations later, one of Elya's descendants breaks the curse and is rewarded with riches. A particularly American kind of folk tale is the tall tale. Tall tales are presented by straight-faced narrators, as humorous but factual, as the stories of Elya and of Katherine Barlow are, and although they contain elements of magic or exaggeration, their narrators seem unaware of these elements. The borderlands between settled land and wilderness in North America were especially fertile ground for the development of these stories, with larger-than-life heroes including Davy Crockett, "King of the Wild Frontier"; Pecos Bill, who tamed the Wild West by lassoing and then riding a tornado; and the superhuman lumberjack Paul Bunyan, whose blue ox was named Babe. These stories captured the imagination of people who thought of the frontier as a wild place where anything could happen, but also as a place that American heroes could tame.

Holes is set in Texas, which, in the days of Kissin' Kate Barlow, was a rough-and-tumble place. Although Katherine Barlow starts out as a mild and pretty schoolteacher, when Sam is killed, she instantly changes into Kissin' Kate, "one of the most feared outlaws in all the West," with the power to control even the rain. Although she is, within the world of the novel, a real person (as Davy Crockett was), she also becomes a legend, with exaggerated stories of her exploits reaching down through the generations to Stanley. Stanley's mother has apparently never believed in the curse or the story of Elya, but Sachar strongly suggests the truth of the story, and points out that "the reader might find it interesting" that the curse—the generations of bad luck that have followed the Yelnats family, despite their good hearts and hard work—ceases to have power over the family the day after Stanley carries Zero up the mountain. By the end of the novel, Stanley's mother may not believe in magic or in curses, but the reader surely does.

Compare & Contrast

- **1880s**: The U.S. Supreme Court upholds the rights of states to prohibit interracial romantic relationships in the 1883 case *Pace v. Alabama*. However, interracial sex or marriage, called miscegenation, is not a crime punishable by death.
  1990s: No states have laws prohibiting relationships between people of different races.
  Today: The Pew Research Center reports that 14.8 percent of couples married in the United States in 2008 were interracial or across ethnic lines, the highest percentage ever recorded.

- **1880s**: There is no separate juvenile justice system in the United States. Children and adults are tried and sentenced in the same courts, and face the same punishments.
  1990s: Alternative detention facilities for juvenile offenders, often called "boot camp detention facilities," are operating in each of the fifty United States.
  Today: Following the 2006 death of

a boy in a Florida boot camp detention facility, such facilities are banned in that state, and many other facilities across the United States have been closed.

- **1880s**: As the narrator points out, there are no telephones to help spread the word that Katherine Barlow and Sam the onion man have been seen kissing.

  1990s: Land line phones are found in nearly every home and building in the United States. The Attorney General uses the phone in the Warden's office to call his own office.

  Today: According to the Federal Communications Commission, there are more than 270 million cell phone subscribers in the United States.

Young Adult Literature in the 1990s

Holes is an example of the literature often called young-adult fiction, or adolescent fiction. Young-adult fiction typically has main characters who are in their teens, and these books are written for—or marketed toward—readers of a similar age. The books may have elements of fantasy or science fiction, but their protagonists and their conflicts are portrayed realistically. Scholars who study young-adult literature, including Michael Cart and others, often refer to S. E. Hinton's *The Outsiders* (1967) as one of the earliest young-adult novels (though others argue for other earlier works, even reaching back as far as Mark Twain's *Huckleberry Finn*, 1884). Before *The Outsiders* and the work of Hinton's contemporaries, including Robert Lipsyte and Robert Cormier, books for young teens tended toward adventure stories, science fiction, and stories of sports heroes, rather than realistic novels about the kinds of problems teens actually face in their lives.

By the 1970s, young-adult literature was well defined, at least by publishers and marketers. Writers sometimes resisted being labeled young-adult authors, fearing that the label would limit their ability to attract adult readers and serious critical attention. Still, a well-defined readership of young people aged twelve to eighteen years old was established, and for nearly all of the decade, young-adult fiction focused on pessimistic portrayals of teens suffering the effects of drug abuse, divorce, depression, friends' suicides, and other traumas. As Cart points out, the 1980s saw a turning away from this gloom with the rise of paperback series novels such as the "Sweet Valley High" series. Although many excellent writers were producing young-adult literature during this period, including Gary Paulsen, Jerry Spinelli, and Cynthia Voigt, the period from the late 1970s through the 1980s is seen as a dull spot in the history of young-adult literature. In an *Orana* essay, critic Mary Owen attributes this to publishers seeming "to want quantity over quality," and observes that "the genre was at risk of dying out."

The middle of the 1990s, however, saw a new energy and a widening readership, what Owen calls "a resurgence and reinvention" of young-adult literature as well as an appeal to readers ranging from as young as twelve to as old as twenty-five. Part of the credit for this expanding audience goes to Philip Pullman's series "His Dark Materials," beginning in 1995, and to J. K. Rowling and her "Harry Potter" series, which first appeared in 1997. Both series were quickly adopted by adults as well as by children—in fact, the Harry Potter books were so popular among adult readers that some of the novels were published in separate editions with cover art deemed more suitable for adults to walk around with. This expanded audience, according to

Cart, "freed authors to tackle more serious subjects and to introduce more complex characters and considerations of ambiguity." Authors were also freed to use a wider variety of narrative techniques. To recognize the high quality of this new age of young-adult fiction, the presenters of the National Book Award established a new category, Young People's Fiction, in 1996, and gave the first award to Victor Martinez for *Parrot in the Oven: Mi Vida*.

Holes, published in 1998, is a prime example of the work coming out of what Cart calls a new "golden age" of young-adult literature. The novel features a teen-aged protagonist, and its characters face real-life issues, including homelessness, poverty, abandonment, and bullying. But like many books of its period, *Holes* is optimistic and hopeful about its characters' chances for a good life. The novel achieved great popularity among young readers, even outside the influence of the classroom, driven in part by the increasing use of the Internet in the late 1990s. The novel's publisher, Scholastic, maintains a *Holes* discussion board online and also has on the Web site an interview with the author based on questions submitted by readers; Sachar also has an active Web site, and there are pages dedicated to him and to the novel on social media sites. But the success of *Holes* is based on quality as well as popularity, as was demonstrated when the book became the third to win the National Book Award for Young People's Literature in 1998.

Holes, Sachar's first young-adult novel after several successful novels for children, was an immediate critical and popular success. Roger Sutton, reviewing the book for *Horn Book*, called it "exceptionally funny, and heart-rending," declaring that "we haven't seen a book with this much plot, so suspensefully and expertly deployed, in too long a time." In *School Library Journal*, Alison Follos called the novel "captivating," "compelling," and "a brilliant achievement." Bill Ott, reviewing *Holes* for *Booklist*, was virtually alone in giving the novel only lukewarm praise, observing that the plot's "mismatched parts don't add up to a coherent whole, but they do deliver a fair share of entertaining and sometimes compelling moments." The novel won the Newbery Medal, the National Book Award, and the *Boston Globe—Horn Book* Award, and was chosen a Best Book of the Year by *Publishers Weekly*, a Best Book for Young Adults by the American Library Association, and a Notable Children's Book of the Year by the *New York Times Book Review*. Interest in the book increased in a second wave in 2003, when the Disney Studios film version of *Holes* was released. The novel has sold millions of copies, and has been adopted for classroom use in middle schools across the country.

Holes has also been analyzed by scholars. Stephanie Yearwood examined the novel's "ontological issues of being and nothingness" in a

2002 essay for *ALAN Review* titled "Popular Postmodernism for Young Adult Readers: *Walk Two Moons, Holes*, and *Monster*." The same year, Pat Pinsent published an essay in *Children's Literature in Education* in which she observed that the novel includes many fairytale elements and "like many fairy tales, it conveys a sense that Fate and Fortune are at work in ensuring the happy ending." Annette Wannamaker, in a 2006 essay for *Children's Literature in Education*, challenges the common view of the novel as a positive view of a young man's maturation, arguing that, "while *Holes* may, on the surface, appear to champion a kinder and gentler version of masculinity, on the level of the subconscious, it champions a … version of boyhood attempting to distance itself from … all things feminine."

What Do I Read Next?

- *Stanley Yelnats' Survival Guide to*

Camp Green Lake (2003) is Sachar's unusual sequel to *Holes*. Narrated by Stanley himself, it offers advice to readers who have been sentenced to spend time at Camp Green Lake, based on new anecdotes from Stanley's time there with Armpit, X-Ray, Zigzag, and the others.

- In a more conventional sequel, *Small Steps* (2008), Sachar follows Armpit and X-Ray, now released from Camp Green Lake, as they try to rebuild their lives.

- In April Henry's *Shock Point* (2006), sixteen-year-old Cassie is sent to a harsh Mexican prison camp for troubled teens to keep her from revealing her stepfather's illegal activities. How she survives the brutal prison and makes her way home to Oregon makes for a thrilling novel.

- Wendelin Van Draanen's *Runaway* (2006) is the story of twelve-year-old Holly, a homeless city girl who keeps a poetry journal as she struggles to find food and shelter and a warm bath.

- Barbara Hayes has collected sixty-eight *Folk Tales and Fables of the World* (2007), beautifully illustrated by Robert Ingpen. The stories come from Africa, Asia, the Americas, Europe, and the Middle East.

- In *True Notebooks: A Writer's Year at Juvenile Hall* (2004), Mark Salzman describes the year he spent teaching a creative writing class in a Los Angeles detention facility for teenage boys who were awaiting trial for serious and violent crimes. The boys' humanity is made vivid through the author's storytelling and through excerpts from their own writing.

- Walter Dean Myers's 2010 novel, *Lock-down*, relates the story of a fourteen-year-old boy who tells, in first-person narration, about his struggle to finish his sentence and then face his future.

- Roger Smith and Marsha McIntosh examine the juvenile justice systems of the United States and Canada in this 2007 nonfiction book, *Youth in Prison*, written specifically for a teen audience.

Sources

Cart, Michael, "From Insider to Outsider: The Evolution of Young Adult Literature," in *Voices from the Middle*, Vol. 9, No. 2, December 2001, pp. 95–97.

Follos, Alison, Review of *Holes*, in *School Library Journal*, Vol. 44, No. 9, September 1998, p. 210.

Genachowski, Julius, "Statement before the U.S. Senate Committee on Commerce, Science and Transportation, Hearing on 'Rethinking the Children's Television Act for a Digital Media Age,'" in *Federal Communications Commission Web site*, July 22, 2009, p. 2, http://hraunfoss.fcc.gov/edocs_public/attachmatch/D 292170A1.pdf (accessed October 1, 2010).

"Juvenile Justice History," in *Center on Juvenile and Criminal Justice*, http://www.cjcj.org/juvenile/justice/juvenile/justice/l (accessed October 1, 2010).

Ott, Bill, Review of *Holes*, in *Booklist*, Vol. 94, No. 19–20, June 1, 1998, p. 1750.

Owen, Mary, "Developing a Love of Reading: Why Young Adult Literature Is Important," in *Orana*, Vol. 39, No. 1, March 2003, http://www.alia.org.au/publishing/orana/39.1/owen.h (accessed October 2, 2010).

"*Pace v. Alabama*, 106 U.S. 583 (1883)," in *Justia.com: U.S. Supreme Court Center*, http://supreme.justia.com/us/106/583/case.html (accessed October 1, 2010).

Passel, Jeffrey S., Wendy Wang, and Paul Taylor, "Marrying Out," in *Pew Research Center*, June 4, 2010, http://pewresearch.org/pubs/1616/american-marriage-interracialinterethnic (accessed October 1, 2010).

Pinsent, Pat, "Fate and Fortune in a Modern Fairy Tale:

Louis Sachar's *Holes*," in *Children's Literature in Education*, Vol. 33, No. 3, September 2002, pp. 203–12.

Sachar, Louis, *Holes*, Farrar, Straus, and Giroux, 1998.

Sutton, Roger, Review of *Holes*, in *Horn Book*, Vol. 74, No. 5, September/October 1998, p. 593.

Wannamaker, Annette, "Reading in the Gaps and Lacks: (De)Constructing Masculinity in Louis Sachar's *Holes*," in *Children's Literature in Education*, Vol. 37, No. 1, March 2006, pp. 15–33.

Yearwood, Stephanie, "Popular Postmodernism for Young Adult Readers: *Walk Two Moons, Holes*, and *Monster*," in *ALAN Review*, Vol. 29, No. 3, Spring/Summer 2002, pp. 50–53.

Further Reading

Greene, Meg, *Louis Sachar*, Rosen, 2004.

This biography, written for middle-school readers, includes an interview with Sachar, a chapter dedicated to *Holes*, and excerpts from *School Library Journal* reviews of other novels by Sachar.

The Newbery and Caldecott Medal Books, 1986–2000: A Comprehensive Guide to the Winners, American Library Association, 2001.

In a section dedicated to *Holes*, this book gathers two reviews, a transcript of Sachar's Newbery Medal acceptance speech, and a biography of the author. Three introductory essays analyze trends in young-adult literature and in the selection of award winners.

Marcus, Leonard S., *Funny Business: Conversations with Writers of Comedy*, Candlewick Press, 2009.

Marcus interviews thirteen writers of humorous books for young readers, including Sachar, Judy Blume, Beverly Cleary, and Christopher Paul Curtis.

Sachar, Sherre, and Carla Sachar, "Louis Sachar,"

in *Horn Book*, Vol. 75, No. 4, July/August 1999, pp. 418–22.

> In this two-part article, Sachar's twelve-year-old daughter, Sherre, and his wife, Carla, describe what it is like to live with the author, and how he balances being famous with being a normal member of a family.

Szalavitz, Maia, *Help at Any Cost: How the Troubled-Teen Industry Cons Parents and Hurts Kids*, Riverhead, 2006.

> This nonfiction book examines various treatment programs for troubled teens, including boot camps in wilderness settings that are intended to rehabilitate strong-willed teens by breaking their spirits. Szalavitz cites research demonstrating that these highly profitable programs are destructive to the teens they are intended to help.

York, Phyllis, David York, and Ted Wachtel, *Toughlove*, Doubleday, 1982.

> After the Yorks decided not to post bail for their troubled daughter after her arrest, they began a movement of parents, adjudicators, and educators that became known as Toughlove. This movement, based on the idea that the best way to deal with destructive behavior begins with

simply not tolerating it, led to the creation of family support groups and residential boot camps for defiant teens.